Meet **M.E**

HAYLEY GREEN

ISBN-13: 9781532932953
ISBN-10: 1532932952

INTRODUCTION

Myalgic Encephalomyelitis is a debilitating neurological disease affecting approximately 250,000 people In the United Kingdom.

It affects men, women and children of all ages. It does not care if you are young or old, rich or poor, an introvert or an extrovert.

M.E affects people of all backgrounds, professions and lifestyles.

This book aims to raise awareness of the condition, and to show that the illness does not discriminate.

CONTENTS

ACKNOWLEDGMENTS

This book is dedicated to all of the M.E sufferers I know. I have not met any of you in person, but you have shown me that there is good to come of everything.

Amongst you I have witnessed the most remarkable strength, bravery and determination through the toughest of struggles.

I can wholeheartedly say that M.E sufferers are amongst some of the most positive people I have come across in my life, and it is this that inspires me to go on in my most difficult times.

Thank you.

Together we are stronger and I have no doubt that we will beat this challenging affliction.

MEET *HAYLEY*

Age: 28

Gender: Female

Age when diagnosed: 23

Occupation when diagnosed: Senior Insurance Sales Advisor

Is your M.E mild, moderate or severe? Moderate

Housebound/Bedbound? 80% Housebound

Hobbies and regular activities before you became ill: Reading, Writing, Eating out, Days out and Socialising.

What do you believe triggered your M.E?

A bout of tonsillitis was the acute trigger which led to my diagnosis in 2011. I had also had Swine flu in 2009 which I feel also contributed. However I believe I was mildly affected for a few years before that, possibly as far back as 2007, but I had no idea what was wrong. I believe ongoing stress and some traumatic events contributed majorly to my deterioration in health.

Who were you officially diagnosed by?

I was diagnosed by a consultant at my local M.E clinic, who was a Rheumatologist.

How long did it take you to get a formal diagnosis?

I was presenting symptoms to my GP for at least four years before I was diagnosed. I mainly felt very exhausted and run down, with enlarged lymph nodes and recurrent viral infections. From there I gradually began to deteriorate and when I caught tonsillitis my health got much worse and I now know I went from mildly, to moderately affected.

This brought me from about 80% of my pre-illness functioning, to around 20%. Five years later i am now only at around 30-40% of my pre-illness level of health.

What were your three most predominant symptoms when you first became unwell?

Fatigue, malaise and severe headaches.

What are your three most predominant symptoms currently?

Pain, orthostatic intolerance and cognitive dysfunction.

Name three things that M.E has taken from you:

My independence, ability to perform simple daily tasks easily – everything takes longer and is painful, from dressing to moving about. Being able to go out without resting in advance (and experiencing payback afterwards) and getting to sleep easily, waking up refreshed the next day.

What has having M.E taught you?

To be grateful for everything I have, because you never know when things can change. I didn't realise just how lucky I was when I was well, but I am now so very grateful for the smallest things in life, that I never even would have noticed before. It has also taught me self-discipline, and that you cannot judge others based purely on 'what you see'.

What is the best piece of advice you have been given?

To be selfish. This may sound like bad advice, but when you lose your health, you can no longer be everything to everyone. I have learnt that health is everything, and although it is still very difficult, you have to put yourself first and do what is best for your health, if you want any chance of getting better.

What is the worst piece of advice you have been given?

To try and push through it. Believe me, in the early days, I did. And I realise now that if I had rested more early on in my illness, I may not be as ill as I am now.

With M.E you HAVE to listen to your body. It is well documented that regular over-exertion can lead to disease progression. You simply cannot 'push through it', as much as you want to - you will just get worse.

A huge part of managing the illness is accepting that you can't do all of the things you could before. I still find that hard at times, but I have most definitely learnt that if I push my body too far, I will pay for it severely.

There are so many things that my mind wants to do, but my body will not comply!

Name three things that you find helps you manage your condition best:

Pacing, adequate rest and a good supplement regime.

If you were well tomorrow, what is one of the first things you would do?

Run! I was never born to be a fitness freak, and before I became unwell, apart from a couple of nights at the gym after work my main source of exercise was walking to work, and dancing all night!But now I get breathless and weak just walking up a flight stairs. I ache to run, to feel free from my body, to feel alive again!

I would love to travel, explore and spend time away from home. Go on days out, and do everything that a lot of people take for granted.

What one thing do you wish people understood about M.E?

That we are unwell 24/7. We may not always look ill, and we may be able to do more on better days. But there are a lot of things you can do 'once', including jumping off cliff! But that doesn't mean we aren't malaised or in pain, we get payback for everything we do.

What you don't see is us laid up in bed after an activity, or unable to move because the pain is so intense. I like to compare my symptoms to air... You can't see them, but they are most definitely there!

Finally, what gives you strength and keeps you going each day?

In one word, gratitude. I have lost a lot through this illness, and experienced some of the worst times of my life. I have lost most of my twenties to it, but out there are children and teenagers suffering.

There are those who are permanently bedbound, those who cannot even see the light of day. And although my life can be hard, I am grateful I have one.

The charity Invest In ME gives me so much hope – there are upcoming medical trials and research and unlike many other conditions, M.E receives very little government funding - leaving sufferers and their friends/families to fund-raise for themselves. If that isn't impressive, I don't know what is!

MEET *CLARE*

Age: 23

Gender: Female

Age when diagnosed: 12

Occupation when diagnosed: High School Student

Is your M.E mild, moderate or severe? Moderate

Housebound/Bedbound? Mostly housebound

Hobbies and regular activities before you became ill: Reading, homework, dancing on the PlayStation 1 Dance Mat.

What do you believe triggered your M.E?

A sinus infection triggered the symptoms which led to my diagnosis but in hindsight I'd had mild symptoms for about four months prior to that after contracting the Norovirus.

Who were you officially diagnosed by?

A Paediatric Rheumatologist.

How long did it take you to get a formal diagnosis?

Four to five months in which time I deteriorated as I was originally diagnosed with Post-viral Fatigue Syndrome within two months of being ill, but was told to keep going to school etc.

What were your three most predominant symptoms when you first became unwell?

Constant headache of varying severity, joint pain, fatigue.

What are your three most predominant symptoms currently?

Joint pain, fatigue, dizziness.

Name three things that M.E has taken from you:

The ability to do simple tasks independently, freedom to go out without feeling awful afterwards, and the ability to think clearly.

What has having M.E taught you?

To be grateful for the things I do have and can do. I never fully appreciated the little things like being able to wash and dress myself until they became big achievements.

What is the best piece of advice you have been given?

To listen to my body and put my health first. It sounds awful but it's the only way there's any hope of seeing improvement.

What is the worst piece of advice you have been given?

To push through the symptoms, and try and continue with a normal life. It doesn't work, in fact it only made things worse. There's so much I want to do but if I do them my symptoms flare drastically.

Name three things that you find helps you manage your condition best:

Pacing, mindfulness and resting.

If you were well tomorrow, what is one of the first things you would do?

Go out and walk by the sea. I used to love walking along the sea front, breathing in the sea air on holidays as a kid. Its something I haven't been able to do since I got ill – wheeling along in a wheelchair isn't quite the same!

What one thing do you wish people understood about M.E?

That it's always there; I may be out looking well but but I am usually hiding a multitude of symptoms, some of which can be severe. You don't see the hours, days or even weeks after when I struggle to move from my bed to the sofa just so I'm on the same floor as the bathroom.

Finally, what gives you strength and keeps you going each day?

Support from friends, family and fellow people with M.E. Without them I honestly don't know how I'd keep going. When everything looks bleak, they're the ones who pick me up, brush me off and help me find a positive and some hope to cling on to. The charity *Invest in ME* also gives me hope in that they are researching the cause in order to find a cure; something we all desperately need.

Meet *KATHRYN*

Age: 37

Gender: Female

Age when diagnosed: 35

Occupation when diagnosed: Despatch/Warehouse worker

Is your M.E mild, moderate or severe? Moderate

Housebound/Bedbound? 50% Housebound

Hobbies and regular activities before you became ill: Dancing around to music with kids, gym, going out for meals, shopping.

What do you believe triggered your M.E?

I am not 100% sure but possibly having my first child... I was never really ill but the timings are correct.

Who were you officially diagnosed by?

My doctor sent me to an M.E clinic where I was officially diagnosed.

How long did it take you to get a formal diagnosis?

I started going to the doctor with symptoms sixteen years prior to my diagnosis.

What were your three most predominant symptoms when you first became unwell?

Exhaustion, mental fatigue, back pain.

What are your three most predominant symptoms currently?

Fatigue, pain all over and cognitive issues (Brain fog/inability to find words)

Name three things that M.E has taken from you:

My freedom to do what I want when I want, and special times with my children.

What has having M.E taught you?

To appreciate the life I do have, even though it's not perfect.

What is the best piece of advice you have been given?

To be selfish, think of what YOU need before others.

What is the worst piece of advice you have been given?

To be honest I don't think I personally have been given any (yet!).

Name three things that you find helps you manage your condition best:

Delegating housework to others too, taking a nap every day and planning well if I need to go out (Ie: resting well before and afterwards).

If you were well tomorrow, what is one of the first things you would do?

Take the dog for a long walk along the beach.

What one thing do you wish people understood about M.E?

It affects me daily and in different ways, and to those who don't know me – don't judge!

Finally, what gives you strength and keeps you going each day?

Seeing my children growing up and doing well at school.

MEET *SANDRA*

Age: 53

Gender: Female

Age when diagnosed: 41

Occupation when diagnosed: Housekeeper/Nanny

Is your M.E mild, moderate or severe? Moderate

Housebound/Bedbound? 50% Housebound

Hobbies and regular activities before you became ill: Walking, socialising, reading, swimming and cycling.

What do you believe triggered your M.E?

I had a flu like virus which never really left me.

Who were you officially diagnosed by?

My G.P.

How long did it take you to get a formal diagnosis?

Twelve months.

What were your three most predominant symptoms when you first became unwell?

Exhaustion, all over body pain, problems concentrating, recurring flu symptoms, severe headaches.

What are your three most predominant symptoms currently?

Fatigue, headaches, pain and poor sleep.

Name three things that M.E has taken from you:

My freedom (I used to drive), my ability to go on long walks with my husband, and most things that I took for granted.

What has having M.E taught you?

To cherish every moment when I am able to be with my family, especially my grandchildren.

What is the best piece of advice you have been given?

To listen to my body although I don't always!

What is the worst piece of advice you have been given?

Get out and walk the hills – get your heart rate up!

Name three things that you find helps you manage your condition best:

Pacing, help from family and patience.

If you were well tomorrow, what is one of the first things you would do?

Go swimming with my grandchildren.

What one thing do you wish people understood about M.E?

That it's not just being tired.

Finally, what gives you strength and keeps you going each day?

My family.

MEET *CHERYL*

Age: 44

Gender: Female

Age when diagnosed: 22

Occupation when diagnosed: Social Work Student

Is your M.E mild, moderate or severe? Currently Moderate, but used to be very Severe

Housebound/Bedbound? Housebound

Hobbies and regular activities before you became ill: Reading, skiing.

What do you believe triggered your M.E?

A virus.

Who were you officially diagnosed by?

My G.P.

How long did it take you to get a formal diagnosis?

A few months.

What were your three most predominant symptoms when you first became unwell?

Nausea, fatigue, flu-like feelings

What are your three most predominant symptoms currently?

Flu like feelings, faintness

Name three things that M.E has taken from you:

Everything.. Even books.

What has having M.E taught you?

That I am stronger than I think, people are not worth bothering with!

What is the best piece of advice you have been given?

To pace myself.

What is the worst piece of advice you have been given?

To exercise!

Name three things that you find helps you manage your condition best:

Pacing and resting.

If you were well tomorrow, what is one of the first things you would do?

I would read.

What one thing do you wish people understood about M.E?

How bad it can get at it's worst. No one 'gets' how anyone can have to stay in bed all day doing absolutely nothing and still be exhausted. At my worst, I was bedbound and unable to do anything for myself. Sometimes even breathing seemed like too much.

Finally, what gives you strength and keeps you going each day?

My faith in God.

MEET *DAWN*

Age: 55

Gender: Female

Age when diagnosed: 48

Occupation when diagnosed: Owner/manager of a children's day nursery

Is your M.E mild, moderate or severe? Moderate to severe

Housebound/Bedbound? Housebound, but spend most of my time on my bed

Hobbies and regular activities before you became ill: Work was my life – I was a manager of a children's nursery, a single mum of six children, I liked eating out, baking shopping and family time.

What do you believe triggered your M.E?

I had an an ear infection and crashed my car, but I believe stress caused a big part, as I had just split up from a very stressful relationship.

Who were you officially diagnosed by?

A consultant.

How long did it take you to get a formal diagnosis?

I went downhill very fast, so it was quick as I changed and became ill almost overnight, I would say three months.

What were your three most predominant symptoms when you first became unwell?

Numbness down the right side of my face and arms, fatigue and a feeling of being spaced out.

What are your three most predominant symptoms currently?

Malaise, pain and brain fog (I still have the numbness, but it is not as bad).

Name three things that M.E has taken from you:

It has taken my independence, work life and being able to have my grandchildren on my own.

What has having M.E taught you?

It has taught me to be patient, to think about my needs, humour – and that one person cannot do everything.

What is the best piece of advice you have been given?

I can't think of one good piece of advice.

What is the worst piece of advice you have been given?

To push myself more.

Name three things that you find helps you manage your condition best:

Pacing, positivity and solitude.

If you were well tomorrow, what is one of the first things you would do?

Go shopping, bake, play with my grandchildren, there would have to be longer than 24 hours in a day!

What one thing do you wish people understood about M.E?

That it's invisible – but whatever I do I am in pain and have constant fatigue. In fact, fatigue isn't the right word for it.

Finally, what gives you strength and keeps you going each day?

Jesus. My belief that in the next world with Jesus, there will be no pain. My children and grandchildren need me, and I might get better. I am very positive and I feel this helps me cope.

Meet *JACK*

Contribution from Mum Michele

Age: 12

Gender: Male

Age when diagnosed: Two days before his 12th birthday

Occupation when diagnosed: Child

Is your M.E mild, moderate or severe? Mild to Moderate

Housebound/Bedbound? Housebound at times

Hobbies and regular activities before you became ill: Out playing with his friends, biking and swimming

What do you believe triggered your M.E?

A virus when he was 8

Who were you officially diagnosed by?

A paediatric doctor at hospital

How long did it take you to get a formal diagnosis?

4 years

What were your three most predominant symptoms when you first became unwell?

Pain all over, fatigue, headaches.

What are your three most predominant symptoms currently?

Pain, tiredness and cognitive dysfunction.

Name three things that M.E has taken from you:

Socialising with his friends, sports and not being able to do the things he used to.

What has having M.E taught you?

To cope with his pains from day to day.

What is the best piece of advice you have been given?

To know his limits but try to keep going.

What is the worst piece of advice you have been given?

To keep active.

Name three things that you find helps you manage your condition best:

Mum and Dads help, and painkillers to help ease the pain.

If you were well tomorrow, what is one of the first things you would do?

To enjoy the life he used to have.

What one thing do you wish people understood about M.E?

That M.E is REAL.

Finally, what gives you strength and keeps you going each day?

Mum, Dad and family help him to get through.

Meet TANYA & Family

Contribution from Tanya

Age: 46

Gender: Female

Age when diagnosed: 46

Occupation when diagnosed: Carer and Housewife

Is your M.E mild, moderate or severe? Moderate

Housebound/Bedbound? Some days housebound on bed or sofa, but other days can venture out.

Hobbies and regular activities before you became ill: Walking the dogs for miles, swimming, reading, zumba and baking.

What do you believe triggered your M.E?

Long term stress due to a number of emotional traumas.

Who were you officially diagnosed by?

First by my G.P who wanted hospital confirmation, and then officially diagnosed by the M.E clinic at the hospital using the Canadian criteria guidelines, and was then confirmed that I had M.E (Not CFS) and possibly arthritis (Need further testing for that.)

How long did it take you to get a formal diagnosis?

About 2/3 years although it was initially labelled a 'stress induced illness' and so went through the therapy and medication route first before finally being listened to when my husband approached my G.P worried about my continuing decline in health.

What were your three most predominant symptoms when you first became unwell?

I became unwell over a period of time, over the past two to three years I have been able to manage less and less until it got to the point I struggle to drive, walk and do household chores etc.

My husband changed my car for an automatic so I can now drive on good days. He has also taken over the shopping as I cannot push the trolley any more. My eldest daughter comes to clean the house when she can as I am unable to do it any more.

Cognitive issues became more apparent, my husband sincerely thought that I was developing Dementia.

I have pain in my muscles and limbs and wear wrist supports as I have no strength in them, lifting a mug is painful. Then there is the awful fatigue and Post-exertional malaise, so I either need Taxi's or a lift out. I am currently applying for a Blue badge.

What are your three most predominant symptoms currently?

The same as above, but anyone who has any knowledge of the illness will know that there are a plethora of symptoms that wax and wane on top of the predominant ones.

Name three things that M.E has taken from you:

My ability to walk the dogs, I can only walk short distances so I am hugely limited although I am too stubborn to use a wheelchair but I do sometimes use crutches. It has taken my ability to read – I struggle to concentrate and end up just re-reading the same paragraph.

And, my freedom to do what I want to do - having to plan how to 'spend' my energy, usually to care for my girls or cook dinner etc.

What has having M.E taught you?

To appreciate the little things and let go of what I cannot control.

What is the best piece of advice you have been given?

To not push through, rest regularly and to accept help.

What is the worst piece of advice you have been given?

To get out and exercise because it's 'all in the mind' and if I tell myself that I am not sick, and exercise I will get better!!

Name three things that you find helps you manage your condition best:

Resting – getting up slowly helps too. I use Voltarol gel like body lotion to take the edge off the pain, and Reflexology when I can afford it. Changing my diet to lactose and gluten free (for me) has helped with some of the digestive issues.

If you were well tomorrow, what is one of the first things you would do?

Go for a long hike with my dogs, read all of the books that are piling up on the table that I am desperate to delve into! Spring clean my house (It's becoming quite of a mess!) and go out with my family.

What one thing do you wish people understood about M.E?

That it affects every part of the body. You have no control over the symptoms and cognitive issues.

Sufferers aren't lazy or faking it – you can be very sick and yet outwardly that may not be apparent. It can affect more than one member of a family, myself and two or three of my daughters have the illness.

It turns your life upside down, and that of those who live with you.

Finally, what gives you strength and keeps you going each day?

The love and support of my family and close friends who understand, and the hope that the charity Invest in ME Research will find treatments which will help sufferers to regain their lives.

Meet *TANYA & Family*

Contribution from Tanya's 2nd born child

Age: 17

Gender: Female

Age when diagnosed: 14

Occupation when diagnosed: Student

Is your M.E mild, moderate or severe? Moderate to Severe

Housebound/Bedbound? Mostly housebound, I was bedbound for the first year with partial paralysis.

Hobbies and regular activities before you became ill: Tag rugby, netball, flash mob dancing and art.

What do you believe triggered your M.E?

Unsure – I had the cervical cancer vaccine followed by viral meningitis and then severe scarlet fever, It was one after the other.

Who were you officially diagnosed by?

Consultant at children's hospital.

How long did it take you to get a formal diagnosis?

Six months – I had two CT scans of my brain and lots of blood tests first, then I was given the M.E diagnosis.

What were your three most predominant symptoms when you first became unwell?

I was unable to walk, and in a wheel chair. I had sensory overload and cognitive issues.

What are your three most predominant symptoms currently?

Pain everywhere, huge fatigue and post-exertional malaise and cognitive issues.

Name three things that M.E has taken from you:

My education, social life and independence.

What has having M.E taught you?

Who my friends are – it turns out that most people can't cope with me being ill. BUT I have discovered photography and art – I had art therapy.

What is the best piece of advice you have been given?

That it's okay to put yourself first and distance yourself from people who drain you.

What is the worst piece of advice you have been given?

To try gradual exercise and Cognitive Behavioural Therapy to train my mind to get better – sadly my sister tried this and it made her more severe so my parents refused.

Name three things that you find helps you manage your condition best:

The use of aids like a shower stool, bed cradle, bean bag trays. Use wheelchair/crutches and wrist/knee supports if they help and keep your head up and make eye contact when people stare - it's a case of regaining control where you can, along with pacing and rest.

If you were well tomorrow, what is one of the first things you would do?

Go to college, attend gigs, travel around the world and train as an art therapist.

What one thing do you wish people understood about M.E?

That it's not a fake illness. It is horrible, painful, isolating and untreatable.

Finally, what gives you strength and keeps you going each day?

My art – it is my therapy. I draw whenever I can because it helps me manage my emotions and focus on something. I hope one, day, to become better so I support the charity Invest In ME Research, as do all my family, and hope they find something.

Meet *TANYA & Family*

Contribution from Tanya's youngest daughter

Age: 16

Gender: Female

Age when diagnosed: 10

Occupation when diagnosed: Student – in my final year at Primary school.

Is your M.E mild, moderate or severe? Moderate/Severe

Housebound/Bedbound? Mostly housebound

Hobbies and regular activities before you became ill: Musical theatre, tap dance, modern dance.

What do you believe triggered your M.E?

I had tonsillitis on ten occasions in twelve months. I ended up being tested for glandular fever when I didn't recover from a bout of tonsillitis. The test was negative.

Who were you officially diagnosed by?

Consultant at children's hospital.

How long did it take you to get a formal diagnosis?

Two months after the negative Glandular fever result.

What were your three most predominant symptoms when you first became unwell?

Narcolepsy, cognitive issues and sensory issues – I couldn't cope with noise, lights or smells.

What are your three most predominant symptoms currently?

Fatigue – (I spend most days in bed) Sore throats and headaches, and pain in joints and muscles.

Name three things that M.E has taken from you:

That no matter how limited your life is, you can still find something to do – and that having one or two close friends is good enough.

What has having M.E taught you?

Who my friends are – it turns out that most people can't cope with me being ill. BUT I have discovered photography and art – I had art therapy.

What is the best piece of advice you have been given?

To rest – stop when I feel tired and remove all negative, daring people from my life.

What is the worst piece of advice you have been given?

To exercise to get better. I was put through gradual exercise therapy and hydrotherapy which made me much worse. Exercise makes your condition more severe – I wish I had known that. I had Cognitive Behavioural Therapy too but for anxiety which was okay, although before that I had a hospital psychiatrist who told me that it was all in my mind. My parents refused to go there again and issued a complaint.

Name three things that you find helps you manage your condition best:

Lots of rest, blackout blinds (and sunglasses when I go out) and avoiding situations where I am prone to sensory overload.

If you were well tomorrow, what is one of the first things you would do?

Go to college, attend gigs, travel – catch up on everything I have missed out on that my friends take for granted.

What one thing do you wish people understood about M.E?

That it' affects anyone. It could be you or someone you love. It is unexpected, life-altering and ruins your life. You can't 'just get better', it isolates you from your peer group and is lonely. I have missed out on so much, and it gets me very down sometimes – I have terrible anxiety and worry about my future.

Finally, what gives you strength and keeps you going each day?

The hope that someday, something will be found to treat this illness. That I can go to college, and try to be a 'normal' teenager.

Meet *OLIVIA*

Age: 20

Gender: Female

Age when diagnosed: 16

Occupation when diagnosed: A-Level Student

Is your M.E mild, moderate or severe? Severe

Housebound/Bedbound? Mostly bedbound. I manage to go out for appointments every now and then, but most of them are house visits – even bed visits now.

Hobbies and regular activities before you became ill: Dancing, acting, photography, going to gigs, hiking, reading books and writing.

What do you believe triggered your M.E?

I had both a virus and the HPV vaccine within the space of for weeks and I never got better. We weren't sure which one it was that made me ill, or whether it was a combination of the two.

Who were you officially diagnosed by?

An M.E Consultant.

How long did it take you to get a formal diagnosis?

Fifteen months.

What were your three most predominant symptoms when you first became unwell?

Fainting, brain fog and post-exertional malaise.

What are your three most predominant symptoms currently?

Fainting, pain and Orthostatic intolerance.

Name three things that M.E has taken from you:

An education, friends and my independence.

What has having M.E taught you?

I've learnt a lot about medical conditions. I appreciate things a lot more. I've learnt to advocate for myself. I've unfortunately learnt about deep suffering.

What is the best piece of advice you have been given?

'Don't be so hard on yourself, you are already trying so hard'. And that even rest is an activity – don't feel guilty.

What is the worst piece of advice you have been given?

I was told that I 'needed to start running and i'll be better'. (I was wheelchair reliant at this point)

Name three things that you find helps you manage your condition best:

I wish I had found things really. I know that a good foundation for me, is a support system and meditating. But that's all I have under my belt at the moment.

If you were well tomorrow, what is one of the first things you would do?

Enroll in a Uni across the country, book a holiday, act in a play. I want to do all things.

What one thing do you wish people understood about M.E?

That I am not going to wake up well tomorrow. Maybe I will have a full recovery, but it'll be a long process, not an overnight thing. I get people still saying to me now that 'It's okay, you might wake up tomorrow and you'll be better'.

Finally, what gives you strength and keeps you going each day?

I want to get better, so much. I have a life to live. I will get to live it.

Meet *JOSIE*

Age: 33

Gender: Female

Age when diagnosed: 23

Occupation when diagnosed: Nursery Nurse

Is your M.E mild, moderate or severe? Severe

Housebound/Bedbound? Bedbound

Hobbies and regular activities before you became ill: Walking, swimming, church activities. GB officer, soloist, youth club leader, Sunday school teacher. Outreach team member, Child evangelism fellowship camp leader.

What do you believe triggered your M.E?

A series of constant infections. I had an infection in some part of my body every couple of weeks for about two years. I seemed to be forever on antibiotics.

Who were you officially diagnosed by?

My GP.

How long did it take you to get a formal diagnosis?

Three years. For a long time the doctor I had seen didn't believe me. It wasn't until my body went into a massive crash and stopped working altogether that a different doctor diagnosed M.E. This was also confirmed later by an M.E specialist.

What were your three most predominant symptoms when you first became unwell?

Fainting, exhaustion and extreme weakness.

What are your three most predominant symptoms currently?

Fainting, exhaustion and extreme weakness although now it has intensified to the point of 'bedboundness'.

Name three things that M.E has taken from you:

My ability to work, my ability to be involved in all of the things I loved to do at church. My whole life – for I was such an active person. One never gets used to the feelings of uselessness that severe M.E brings.

What has having M.E taught you?

That I have worth as a person for who I am not just for the things that I can do physically.

What is the best piece of advice you have been given?

To never ever ever ever let go of of the better day, now matter how 'black' things get.

What is the worst piece of advice you have been given?

To push yourself to the limits – in doing so my body only deteriorated.

Name three things that you find helps you manage your condition best:

Painkillers for the headaches. Cutting out dairy products has got the IBS symptoms under control, and taking garlic capsules every day to strengthen the immune system.

If you were well tomorrow, what is one of the first things you would do?

Go for a run around the fields to celebrate a body that actually works! :-)

What one thing do you wish people understood about M.E?

That it is a really serious illness like M.S and Cancer. People think that it's just being a wee bit tired but it totally and utterly takes over ones life and stops one from living a 'normal life'.

Finally, what gives you strength and keeps you going each day?

My faith in the Lord. He gives me the strength to get through one day at a time and continue to believe for a breakthrough.

Meet *CHLOE*

Age: 23

Gender: Female

Age when diagnosed: 23

Occupation when diagnosed: Staff Nurse on a very busy major trauma unit, with lots of night shifts and long hours.

Is your M.E mild, moderate or severe? Mostly moderate, mild on my better days.

Housebound/Bedbound? Housebound 50-60% of the time.

Hobbies and regular activities before you became ill:I really was a social butterfly before I got ill. I loved my life. Work hard, play hard was my motto.

I regularly went out clubbing a socialising with my friends. I worked out regularly at the gym. I really enjoyed body combat and body pump and dancing classes. I tried to pack as much into my day as I possibly could. I was the agony aunt of my friends, always there for them when they needed me.

What do you believe triggered your M.E?

A bad episode of glandular fever also known as the Epstein-Barr virus which I was hospitalised with at the beginning of 2015. I have also had a lot of trauma in the past 5 years including delayed grief - as I had not emotionally dealt with the death of my dad when I was 11 years old.

I was also in a damaging relationship and dealt with the break up with that. My perfectionism and ambitious personality meant that I always pushed myself too hard.

My health was never fully right since I had the Hepatitis B vaccination which I was expected to have when I began my nursing degree in 2010. I had a very bad reaction to it and it has left me with permanent nausea since then. The more I learn about my M.E and the more I learn I believe that this may have been a contributing factor.

Who were you officially diagnosed by?

I was officially diagnosed by one of the Occupational health doctors at the hospital where I was working. My GP is really good ans supportive but still continues to say that it is just the glandular fever virus / post-viral fatigue. He does not like me to use the word M.E or CFS.

How long did it take you to get a formal diagnosis?

I was lucky to get a formal diagnosis in 8 months approx, unlike some poor sods who wait years being made to feel like it is 'all in their heads'.

What were your three most predominant symptoms when you first became unwell?

Muscle pain, debilitating fatigue, poor concentration, swollen glands and sore throats.

What are your three most predominant symptoms currently?

Fatigue, headaches that are rarely relived by analgesics, muscle pain (Mainly in my legs) and twitching. I also suffer from brain fog at times.

Name three things that M.E has taken from you:

My spontaneity, my 'joie de vivre' attitude towards life and my confidence.

What has having M.E taught you?

It has taught me what true love really is. I know that sounds soppy, but I had only been seeing my partner for a few months before I was struck down with M.E. We went from the 'honeymoon period' of the relationship, to glandular fever and M.E. It has not been easy but he has stayed with me and been there for me both physically and emotionally. He always manages to make me laugh.

What is the best piece of advice you have been given?

To stop putting on a brave face – be assertive and selfish at times. Your friends etc aren't the ones who are crying in pain and cant sleep the next night or move off the sofa for days.

What is the worst piece of advice you have been given?

Basically that it was 'all in my head' and if I thought positively it would 'go away'.

Name three things that you find helps you manage your condition best:

Pacing, CBT (I have the most amazing understanding Psychologist who I see through Occupational health), relaxation and meditation.

If you were well tomorrow, what is one of the first things you would do?

Go for a run around the beach feeling free and go dancing.

What one thing do you wish people understood about M.E?

That having a nap does not help!!! REGULAR TIREDNESS IS NOT THE SAME AS M.E.

That people with me are not just being 'precious' and attention seeking. People who do not have M.E do not realise what a struggle through the day really is. They don't see that meeting for a coffee (sitting down) or even having a long chat on the phone at times takes serious motivation, energy and effort.

Keeping afloat the dark pool of M.E is is bloody damn hard. Just because we don't have anything to show for it such as a cast or no hair etc, this means that it must be 'all in our heads' and the pain we feel doesn't really exist. This is one of the most hurtful parts of this illness!

Finally, what gives you strength and keeps you going each day?

That there will be a cure one day and the old Chloe (With new found wisdom of course, ha-ha) can slowly emerge from the dark pool of M.E. My spirit and sense of humour get me through the day, even the very difficult ones.

Meet *IMOGEN*

Age: 34

Gender: Female

Age when diagnosed: 30

Occupation when diagnosed: Community Mental Health Support Worker

Is your M.E mild, moderate or severe? At best moderate, at worst severe

Housebound/Bedbound? I have times when I am house and bed bound but I do make it out about once a week. I use a wheelchair sometimes, as cannot walk far.

Hobbies and regular activities before you became ill: Playing bass guitar and cello, socialising, going to concerts, Zumba and countryside walks.

What do you believe triggered your M.E?

A virus which I contracted in 2010. It made me so ill that my GP admitted me to hospital.

Who were you officially diagnosed by?

An occupational health doctor at work, and I am eternally grateful to him.

How long did it take you to get a formal diagnosis?

Over 2 years.

What were your three most predominant symptoms when you first became unwell?

Vomiting, severe pain and inability to tolerate sensory stimuli.

What are your three most predominant symptoms currently?

Pain, Orthostatic intolerance, feeling poisoned.

Name three things that M.E has taken from you:

My mobility, my social life and my confidence.

What has having M.E taught you?

How to be strong in the face of huge adversity, who my real friends are to be grateful for what I do have left.

What is the best piece of advice you have been given?

Being taught how to pace.

What is the worst piece of advice you have been given?

To just 'push through' the symptoms.

Name three things that you find helps you manage your condition best:

Pacing, pain relief and my loving, supportive diamond of a husband.

If you were well tomorrow, what is one of the first things you would do?

Something active!!

What one thing do you wish people understood about M.E?

Just because we can do something one day, doesn't mean that we can do the same activity every day. There is often a price we pay for over-exerting ourselves that you don't see. It involves intense suffering that would be hard for a healthy person to comprehend.

Finally, what gives you strength and keeps you going each day?

My husband – who is my rock and my best friend. I couldn't do it without him!

Meet *PAT*

Age: 57

Gender: Female

Age when diagnosed: 55

Occupation when diagnosed: Branch administrator for a trade union

Is your M.E mild, moderate or severe? Moderate to Severe

Housebound/Bedbound?Housebound 90% of the time and bedbound for 60% of that.

Hobbies and regular activities before you became ill: Hiking, browsing vintage fairs and antique shops, knitting, reading, computer programming and just going out and about with my husband and friends.

What do you believe triggered your M.E?

I had swine flu very badly in 2012, which I believe triggered the Epstein-Barr virus left over from glandular fever years ago – exacerbated by several years of personal stress. Note that my diagnosis date is different, I believe I had it for years before I was officially diagnosed.

Who were you officially diagnosed by?

An M.E consultant at the hospital.
How long did it take you to get a formal diagnosis?

A year.

What were your three most predominant symptoms when you first became unwell?

Fatigue, brain fog and P.E.N.E (Post-exertional Neuro-immune exhaustion)

What are your three most predominant symptoms currently?

Muscle weakness, fatigue and sensitivity to noise and light.

Name three things that M.E has taken from you:

Walking in the Yorkshire hills, my ability to be spontaneous and my enthusiasm for work.

What has having M.E taught you?

To ditch 'toxic' people and to cherish those who are not.

What is the best piece of advice you have been given?

Pacing.

What is the worst piece of advice you have been given?

Also pacing. Pacing is undoubtedly really really useful, and it is essential I think to reduce exhaustion, especially in the early days or with mild ME.

But, and this is the 'worst piece of advice' bit - it spoils things, you can't be spontaneous any more, sporting events and theatre attendance, concerts etc are very difficult. Some of us naughty peeps with ME ahem ignore It and take the PENE afterwards as part and parcel of the activity.

Name three things that you find helps you manage your condition best:

Enough time to rest, mobility aids (Scooter, wheelchair, cane) and PIP (Personal Independence Payment) money so that I can afford a person to clean the house.

If you were well tomorrow, what is one of the first things you would do?

Book a holiday somewhere with wonderful scenery so that I could go walking, or riding even.

What one thing do you wish people understood about M.E?

That even if we don't look sick – we are.

Finally, what gives you strength and keeps you going each day?

My husband, grand-babies and appreciating the little things in life.

Meet *JOSEPH*

Age: 33

Gender: Male

Age when diagnosed: 38

Occupation when diagnosed: Supporting people with disabilities into employment

Is your M.E mild, moderate or severe? Moderate

Housebound/Bedbound? Neither

Hobbies and regular activities before you became ill: Kung fu teacher, actor and musician, performing regularly in plays, martial arts demonstrations and playing at festivals and gigs.

What do you believe triggered your M.E?

In 2008 I had glandular fever, which I didn't take time to recover from – this was followed by a severe emotional breakdown six months later, followed by Bronchitis. In April 2009 I was diagnosed with Hashimoto's Hypothyroidism.

Who were you officially diagnosed by?

South Coast Chronic Fatigue in April 2011.

How long did it take you to get a formal diagnosis?

Nearly three years from the onset of my fatigue.

What were your three most predominant symptoms when you first became unwell?

Fatigue, shortness of breath and 'looping thoughts' anxiety.

What are your three most predominant symptoms currently?

Fatigue, muscle pain and intolerance of emotional stress.

Name three things that M.E has taken from you:

Friends, success and head-flips. Socialising takes too much energy and I have had to avoid promotion to keep my stress levels down.

I also went from being 'super human' – being able to impress people with head-flips, no-handed cartwheels and and flying kicks. Now I am envious of people who can go for afternoon walks.

What has having M.E taught you?

Don't do too much. If I had of paced myself and taken time to recover when I was healthy then I would have recovered from a healthy body, instead of pushing a body struggling to cope with illness to breaking point and now I am unable to recover.

What is the best piece of advice you have been given?

Don't try and get back to who I was before. I did far too much and didn't stop. To learn to be someone who doesn't do too much and recognise when to stop and rest before it's too late.

What is the worst piece of advice you have been given?

Before I was fully diagnosed a doctor told me to drink sports drinks to improve my energy levels, they didn't help and I quickly gained weight that I couldn't shift.

Graded exercise therapy was also bad, in the way it was described to me but I have found my own way with it which includes listening to my body when I know I shouldn't do it.

I caught a cold last week and instantly decided that I needed a week off exercising so that I could fully recover. I was able to exercise fully again today and I have adjusted my target to accommodate the weeks rest I have had.

Name three things that you find helps you manage your condition best:

Relaxation and mindfulness. I am rubbish at them although I meditated easily all the time before I was ill but these do help and when I can do them the results are brilliant.

I saw a brilliant Psychotherapist (I was seeing them for Post-traumatic stress disorder) who taught me the difference between the two and gave me a wonderful library of recordings to listen to.

I see a Chiropractor who has managed to sort out my muscular and skeletal problems. She encouraged me to stretch gently and daily (when I can of course) and now most of the pain I had before is under control or gone altogether.

Gentle stretching is so important because the muscles can get so stiff and achy – it helps with posture and alignment too. Chiropractors aren't cheap but they are worth every penny if you get a good one. After my first session I felt like I had a new back and after the following weeks I felt like I had been given new arms, legs and neck. That's not something you can put a price tag on. In my opinion Chiropractors should be available on the NHS.

Stretching followed by Graded exercise therapy in my own way. I took the principle of building up by 10% every two weeks and started with ten repetitions of a simple exercise with no weights. After two weeks I added another repetition and after another two weeks I added another. I'm now up to 59 repetitions two or five times a week and I only increase when I feel confident to go a biy further after two weeks. If i've had a busy day, no exercise. If I am ill, no exercise. If, for no reason, my body says "We're not doing it today" I agree and rest.

If you were well tomorrow, what is one of the first things you would do?

I would keep using relaxation, mindfulness, the chiropractor and still follow my own way of GET because that's who I want to be, even when I'm well. The main difference would be that rest would be a choice and a reward.

What one thing do you wish people understood about M.E?

Don't give up looking for answers and solutions - in November 2015, after five and half years of everything being tested, I sat in front of an Endocrinologist who went through all my test results telling me they were all normal or better.

At the end I asked "What else?". He responded that I could be tested for Vitamin D, I was tested and they found I was deficient and I started on Vitamin D supplements a week later.

I had already met the criteria for being referred to ME specialists twice in five years, had countless specialist appointments but it was this one Endocrinologist who took my "What's next?" question seriously. In two weeks' time I'll be retested and find out if I'm on the right dose.

Finally, what gives you strength and keeps you going each day?

That's the strangest question because I don't know what kept me going before I had the Vitamin D test. Now I have some hope but before that test I was convinced they'd never find anything and there would be no cure.

Something kept me going and I'm really glad it did. Now I've cracked GET, found mindfulness and have some hope from Vitamin D I have things to aim for and the light at the end of the tunnel probably isn't a train.

Meet *SAMINA*

Age: 25

Gender: Female

Age when diagnosed: 25

Occupation when diagnosed: Criminology & Psychological Science student at the Open University

Is your M.E mild, moderate or severe? Mild for several years, moderate for around 3 years and it fluctuates from moderate to severe for the last 18 months/2 years. I do venture out some days but only for short periods of time, usually tired throughout whatever I'm doing when out.

Housebound/Bedbound? On bad days I am housebound and bedbound

Hobbies and regular activities before you became ill: Going to the gym everyday and doing Thai boxing. Going on holidays, socialising and arts & crafts, walking my dog, going out for dinner, A day out shopping, reading lots.

What do you believe triggered your M.E?

A viral infection from an operation when I was younger.

Who were you officially diagnosed by?

An Immunologist.

How long did it take you to get a formal diagnosis?

Around ten years.

What were your three most predominant symptoms when you first became unwell?

Fatigue unusual for a teenager, severe muscle pain and sleep dysfunction.

What are your three most predominant symptoms currently?

Sleep dysfunction & severe exhaustion. Memory & Cognitive dysfunction. Severe bone & muscle pain that made me suicidal.

Name three things that M.E has taken from you:

My independence and spontaneity, my confidence & self esteem, and my dreams I had of a career & travelling.

What has having M.E taught you?

It's definitely taught me who my friends are & to remove negative/draining people from my life. To never take anything for granted and it's taught me to realise how strong I can be. It's also taught me it's okay to say no and put myself (and my health) first.

What is the best piece of advice you have been given?

Take each day as it comes. You never know what's around the corner.

What is the worst piece of advice you have been given?

Don't sleep as much, eat better & "it could be worse".

Name three things that you find helps you manage your condition best:

Positivity. Resting when needed, including not being embarrassed when I have to use my wheelchair or crutches. Talking with other sufferers and high dose morphine patches plus liquid morphine.

If you were well tomorrow, what is one of the first things you would do?

Take my dog for a run! Finish university & follow my dream job. Book a holiday, read lots of books without cognitive dysfunction.

See my friends knowing I wouldn't let them down & join the gym again. I'd also do all the things healthy people can take for granted like having a shower without needing a nap!

What one thing do you wish people understood about M.E?

How serious & debilitating it is. It's like air - you can't see it but it's there 24/7.

 I wish people were more aware about the disease & knew we weren't lazy, and when I cancel plans it's nothing personal, it just means I can't function enough to hold a conversation of any kind.

I'm not the person I used to be. I'm forever changing due to the disease.

Finally, what gives you strength and keeps you going each day?

My dog, the ME forum, talking to God/praying, listening to music when I drive, my friends & family that support me, and a hope of a treatment or cure for ME.

Meet *HANNA*

Age: 44

Gender: Female

Age when diagnosed: 43

Occupation when diagnosed: Human Resources Director

Is your M.E mild, moderate or severe? Mild to moderate

Housebound/Bedbound? Rarely

Hobbies and regular activities before you became ill: Gym, socialising and travel.

What do you believe triggered your M.E?

A near fatal car accident in 1998 and subsequent countless very stressful

Who were you officially diagnosed by?

Bath Mineral Hospital.

How long did it take you to get a formal diagnosis?

Since 1998, back and forth to many GP's in Aberdeen, Cornwall and then finally Wiltshire before my current GP recognised what was going on.

What were your three most predominant symptoms when you first became unwell?

Fatigue, cognitive issues and sleeplessness.

What are your three most predominant symptoms currently?

The same, but on a far less severe scale.

Name three things that M.E has taken from you:

The ability to be spontaneous.

What has having M.E taught you?

To nurture myself.

What is the best piece of advice you have been given?

To pace and be 'selfish'.

What is the worst piece of advice you have been given?

To 'push on through', 'get it sorted' or I won't be seen as credible in my job....

Name three things that you find helps you manage your condition best:

Pacing, relaxation and being selfish about my energy.

If you were well tomorrow, what is one of the first things you would do?

Start getting fit again! Take the dogs out for a long walk.

What one thing do you wish people understood about M.E?

That it is serious and debilitating. Its invisible but not to the person dealing with it.

Finally, what gives you strength and keeps you going each day?

My husband and our dogs. And proving my boss wrong!!

Meet *NIKKI*

Age: 33

Gender: Female

Age when diagnosed: 32

Occupation when diagnosed: I haven't been able to work for almost 4 years due to ill health.

Is your M.E mild, moderate or severe? Moderate/Severe

Housebound/Bedbound? Mostly housebound, occasionally bedbound

Hobbies and regular activities before you became ill: Reading, writing, drawing, socialising, watching live bands, arts & crafts, karaoke, dancing, playing guitar, walking, swimming.

What do you believe triggered your M.E?

My health deteriorated rapidly after giving birth to my son in 2011. It was extremely traumatic and I believe that was the trigger. However, I had swine flu in 2009 and often wonder if there is a connection.

Who were you officially diagnosed by?

A consultant at the CF clinic in Salford diagnosed me and then sent me on my way with no further support.

How long did it take you to get a formal diagnosis?

Almost 4 years. I originally went to my GP with severe back and pelvic pain. Other symptoms soon followed, including fatigue and memory problems. It was put down to anxiety and depression so I was sent for CBT and put on antidepressants.

What were your three most predominant symptoms when you first became unwell?

Pain, general fatigue, cognitive dysfunction.

What are your three most predominant symptoms currently?

Pain, post exertional neuro-immune exhaustion (PENE) and cognitive dysfunction .

Name three things that M.E has taken from you:

I had to stop studying towards my degree as i can't concentrate for long or remember anything I've learned. All that hard work for nothing.

I can no longer go and watch live bands due to sensory overload and the fact that most music venues are not disabled friendly.

But the worst thing ME has taken from me is the chance to be the mother I always thought I'd be. I have a 4 year old son that I can't play with or even take to school in the mornings without payback. That's the hardest thing.

What has having M.E taught you?

Not to judge others who 'don't look sick'. There are so many invisible illnesses out there and until you've walked a mile in someone else's shoes, you have no idea what they have to battle on a daily basis.

What is the best piece of advice you have been given?

To listen to my body and learn to say NO.

What is the worst piece of advice you have been given?

To just push through it. I did try that at first when I was only mildly affected and things only got worse. I now know (from research and from personal experience) that you cannot simply 'push through' this disease.

The main symptom that distinguishes ME from other, similar illnesses is Post-exertional neuroimmune exhaustion / malaise (PENE / PEM). If I'd rested more in those early days, I probably wouldn't be this badly affected now.

Name three things that you find helps you manage your condition best:

Adequate rest, pacing and keeping stress to a minimum.

If you were well tomorrow, what is one of the first things you would do?

I would take my little boy to the park and play for hours!

What one thing do you wish people understood about M.E?

That it isn't just fatigue and it isn't psychological! It's a serious, physical illness that, as yet has no cure. The most severely affected are bedbound and tube fed. People have died from ME. Until people realise that (especially our doctors) there will never be any progress.

Finally, what gives you strength and keeps you going each day?

My gorgeous little boy and my wonderful, supportive and understanding partner. Without him I would be in a much worse condition. I would be lost.

Meet *MAKAYLA*

Age: 12 (8 when first ill)

Gender: Female

Age when diagnosed: 8

Occupation when diagnosed: Child

Is your M.E mild, moderate or severe? Moderate

Housebound/Bedbound? Neither

Hobbies and regular activities before you became ill: Baton twirling, Swimming (twice a week) Horse riding, Youth club, Dancing - ballet and tap

What do you believe triggered your M.E?

Shingles in August, then became ill in September

Who were you officially diagnosed by?

A Paediatrician at Bristol Childrens Hospital

How long did it take you to get a formal diagnosis?

5 months.

What were your three most predominant symptoms when you first became unwell?

Tiredness, pain and sore throat.

What are your three most predominant symptoms currently?

Tiredness, pain and brain fog.

Name three things that M.E has taken from you:

Horse riding - I do still do it but nowhere near as much as i would like to, i would like to do pony club, camps, competitions.

What has having M.E taught you?

That I can do stuff but I have to take it easy.

What is the best piece of advice you have been given?

To listen to my body and learn to say NO.

What is the worst piece of advice you have been given?

Hospital said "In 3 years time it will all be a distant memory"...4 years and 4 months later it's still not a distant memory - still in the nightmare.

Name three things that you find helps you manage your condition best:

Medical herbalist medication, pacing and an understanding school.

If you were well tomorrow, what is one of the first things you would do?

Ride my horse all day and not just for a hour which i'm only allowed, spend the day riding and being at the yard.

What one thing do you wish people understood about M.E?

How it makes you feel.

Meet *BILL*

Age: 59

Gender: Male

Age when diagnosed: 49

Occupation when diagnosed: Administration Manager

Is your M.E mild, moderate or severe? Moderate in the main but Severe in the sensory elements of the illness.

Housebound/Bedbound? Mostly housebound, occasionally bedbound

Hobbies and regular activities before you became ill:
Marathon running, Archery, Badminton, Coaching and Managing a girls football team.

Bill Say's:

I think it's very important that we do what we can within our limited energy resources to raise ME Awareness as little is done outside of the ME community to do so. With my
10th Anniversary of living with ME having just passed, whilst we need to help and support each other, I see that it's more vital than ever to ensure than we aim our energies outwards to those who don't know, but need to know

about ME. We need to be aiming at those who can make a difference.

 I do that partly using an ME site as a base. Whilst www.York-ME-Community.org is used to support the local community, it also has a link to **Invest in ME** as I can see the great work they are doing for us and want to spread the word ! They support the areas of research that I can see being useful to us, now and in the future.

 I am working to bring local groups, sports clubs and businesses on board through giving talks on ME to raise further awareness, and am in regular contact with a group of MP's of various parties bringing them up to speed with the latest goings on in the ME Community. Using the local press and radio also helps raise awareness in the York area.

 Many with ME are too ill to do much to raise awareness, but if everybody, that's sufferers, carers, family and friends could tell just one new person a month about ME, just think of the difference that could make. We may have ME, but ME doesn't have us!

ME and My 'Friend'

I want to Chat
And things like that
Like we used to do
It hurts to talk
It pains to walk
But I'll get myself to you.

I'll get there, it's not that far
Travel by bus, too tough by car
Vibrations turn senses into mire
The slightest bump, the more I tire
Noise and sounds care not for bounds
Twist my senses and my blood
Turn brain cells into mud

So tired now my jaw grows numb
I slur my words, It's so absurd
I sound like a drunken bum
Not there yet, a bit to go
Bus on time
But seems so slow
Traffic stops at another junction
More of my body
Ceases to function.

Came this way when we used to run
Used to chat, used to have fun
Another lifetime ago that was
We'd run for charity, we had clarity
And a noble, worthwhile cause
Runs became less
Health was a mess
You did them on your own

You'd keep in touch, then not so much
A quick chat on the phone

At least today
You've said we'd meet
The coffee shop
Bottom of the street
Bus pulls in
Feeling grim
But got here all the same
Feel so weak, hard to speak
The journey's been a drain.

You're not there
The chair sits spare
No message left, feel bereft
It seems you didn't care

Of friends I had
You were the best
Through thick and thin
You stood the test
But somewhere through this tougher time
Somewhere it seems you lost your spine
One more thing to see decline
I thought you were a friend of mine

I haven't lost you
You've lost me
You are just too blind to see
I will be stronger, will look back no longer
Through this, my fight with M.E

Life moves on
Now you've gone
I am stronger, not forlorn

We need real friends, not just pretends
To tell this beast, the war is on.

By Bill Clayton.

ME ISN'T REAL YOU KNOW……

ME isn't real you know
ME is all just fake
I chose to give up work you know
To rely upon the state

ME isn't real you know
It's all just in my mind
I just fancied giving up
On everything in my life

ME isn't real you know
ME is all just talk
I just chose to give up running
And use a stick to help me walk

ME isn't real you know
The pain is in my head
In fact it's also in my arms
My back, my ribs, my legs

ME isn't real you say
It's all just my pretend
You think I choose, my life to lose
As well as my final friend?

ME isn't real you say
Laziness is in my genes
You say this though not knowing
That I've worked since in my teens

ME is just fake you say
I really am ok
Do you really reckon, for just one second
I'd choose to be this way?

Lazy sod, it's in your head
Wish I could just stay in bed
Shake it off, stop complaining
To be like that, you must be feigning

Just not possible, to have pain like that
And legs that just won't go
To feel battered and bruised like you say you are
You're a lying so and so......

To be this way is not by choice,
To hide from light, to hide from noise,
Friends don't call, and that's not all
They talk behind our back
They say we're no fun, won't go for a run
But then they don't know Jack.

Hit with this, we don't know why
Keep fighting on, is our battle cry
All we ask for is belief,
It's taken our lives like a skulking thief

I ask for not a single pound
But when next the thought is going round
Let's all do a charity run
What's our cause, is there one?
Can I ask that you keep minds free
And choose to help those with ME.

By Bill Clayton

E MOT

Woke up today
It's not gone away
This beast, it's here for good
Thought maybe a dream
But a nightmare it seems
I'd sleep through it all if I could.

As another day dawns
There's something more going on
The pain's a bit harder to stand
It's tougher to face, when it's in a new place
Again, just forget what you've planned.

This pain, it's not mine
It's all down my spine
I've not had it just there before
But is it worth going sick
And risk another big kick
When you walk through the surgery door.

Being told it's baloney,
That you're just such a phoney
You think twice about seeing the doc
We've enough going on, so we'll leave it alone
Rather than risk yet another big knock.

Over the years, I've crunched through my gears
I know I'm battered and bruised
I'm the broken toy in the toy box
My body's been well over used
But we must be aware
When it's not wear and tear
We must not let that confuse.

Don't take it for granted
It's something you've landed
While your system's been running so low
Could just be an ache, but a major mistake
To ignore it and just let it go.
Not all things you see, are tied to ME
Don't forget other ills do abound
It'd just be our luck, we've forgotten to duck
When they've been handed around.

It's easy to do
Just ignoring a clue
Others have pain 'just like that'
It's a tug, it's a pull

It's a new kid in school
But don't use the welcoming mat.

Ring the GP, for your own MOT
Get checked out to see that you're fine
We know we're not well, but never can tell
Don't ignore an obvious sign.

Don't be swayed, or even delayed
Though you'll be chuffed to bits you'll see
Having been given every scan,
Known to woman or man
To be told it's only ME !

By Bill Clayton

MY M.E. STORM
I can feel the storm clouds forming
All around my head

I should have stopped my 'doing'
And rested more instead.

The soft patter of the raindrops
That turn into a thud
As my mind it slows as the downpour grows
Turning every thought to mud

My scrambled brain
Is like thundering rain
I cower from the merest light
Like a laser beam, that noxious stream
Makes me hide from its line of sight

The wind gathers pace
As it reaches my face
It locks my jaw in jail
Words cannot be formed
Nerve ends are stormed
In a batter of blistering hail

The rumble of thunder
Soon drives me under
My senses are now so inviting,
The noise of a page, as it turns, causes rage
Like being hit by a bolt of lightning.

The darkening skies, have closed my eyes
Caused my limbs to spasm
From thought to deed,
My body concedes
Is forged an unbridgeable chasm.

Can't take in the spoken word
Just makes no sense, so absurd
Simple chat I have to concede
Rolls over me, like tumbleweed.
Not just tiredness,
Not just fatigue,
This is in a different league
These storms are causing me to drown

I can feel my body closing down

I know in time the sun will shine
We'll see the shoots of Spring
But a wind of change is what we need
To help us beat this thing

We won't go under,
Without causing some thunder
A volcano of hot angry fire
We'll rise as one voice,
making some noise

Awareness is what we desire.
I know that together,
We can change this bad weather
So let's be in it as one
Let's keep up the fight, with all of our might
And we'll enjoy our day in the sun.

By Bill Clayton

Here are some excerpts from the Invest In M.E website which contain valuable information on the illness from a credible source.

Have you heard of M.E?

One may read or hear that there is little known about the cause of M.E and that there are different opinions on the causes.
To sufferers and carers/parents of sufferers these opinions do not coincide with reality.

A lot is known about Neurological Myalgic Encephalomyelitis (ME)
The opinions of those suffering is quite clear – this is an organic illness.

Invest In M.E will join the many other organisations which are now campaigning for bio-medical research into ME so that little doubt will remain that this is a biological illness which can only be treated and cured by Science.

M.E Facts

The first clinically documented outbreak of M.E in the UK was in 1955 at the Royal Free Hospital where Dr. Ramsey noted the symptoms that would lead to a definition of M.E, although historical figures such as Florence Nightingale are believed to have suffered from this illness *and mention of M.E in medical literature goes back as far as the 1930's.*

M.E Statistics

There are over 250,000 sufferers of M.E in the UK (at a conservative estimate) with around 25% being classified as being severely affected (Ie Bedbound or Housebound)

How serious is ME?

ME is a serious neurological illness. It exhibits a number of symptoms (described below). The severity of the illness can depend on many things with some sufferers outwardly leading near normal lives and others being severely incapacitated, bed-bound and unable to care for themselves.

A patient with ME/CFS will meet the criteria for fatigue, post-exertional malaise and/or fatigue, sleep dysfunction, and pain; have two or more neurological/cognitive manifestations and one or more symptoms from two of the categories of autonomic, neuroendocrine and immune manifestations; and adhere to item 7. (from Canadian Guidelines definitions)

1. *Fatigue:* The patient must have a significant degree of new onset, unexplained, persistent, or recurrent physical and mental fatigue that substantially reduces activity level.

2. *Post-Exertional Malaise and/or Fatigue:* There is an inappropriate loss of physical and mental stamina, rapid muscular and cognitive fatigability, post exertional malaise and/or fatigue and/or pain and a tendency for other associated symptoms within the patient's cluster of symptoms to worsen. There is a pathologically slow recovery period—usually 24 hours or longer.

3. *Sleep Dysfunction:* There is unrefreshed sleep or sleep quantity or rhythm disturbances such as reversed or chaotic diurnal sleep rhythms.

4. *Pain:* There is a significant degree of myalgia. Pain can be experienced in the muscles and/or joints, and is often widespread and migratory in nature. Often there are significant *headaches* of new type, pattern or severity.

5. _Neurological/Cognitive Manifestations_: _Two or more_ of the following difficulties should be present: confusion, impairment of concentration and short-term memory consolidation, disorientation, difficulty with information processing, categorizing and word retrieval, and perceptual and sensory disturbances–e.g., spatial instability and disorientation and inability to focus vision. Ataxia, muscle weakness and fasciculations are common. There may be overload1 phenomena: cognitive, sensory–e.g., photophobia and hypersensitivity to noise–and/or emotional overload, which may lead to "crash"2 periods and/or anxiety. _Carruthers et al. 11_

6. _At Least One Symptom from Two of the Following Categories_:
a. Autonomic Manifestations: orthostatic intolerance–neurally mediated hypotenstion (NMH), postural orthostatic tachycardia syndrome (POTS), delayed postural hypotension; light-headedness; extreme pallor; nausea and irritable bowel syndrome; urinary frequency and bladder dysfunction; palpitations with or without cardiac arrhythmias; exertional dyspnea.
b. Neuroendocrine Manifestations: loss of thermostatic stability– subnormal body temperature and marked diurnal fluctuation, sweating episodes, recurrent feelings of feverishness and cold extremities; intolerance of extremes of heat and cold; marked weight change–anorexia or abnormal appetite; loss of adaptability and worsening of symptoms with stress.
c. Immune Manifestations: tender lymph nodes, recurrent sore throat, recurrent flu-like symptoms, general malaise, new sensitivities to food, medications and/or chemicals.

7. _The illness persists for at least six months_. It usually has a distinct onset,** although it may be gradual. Preliminary diagnosis may be possible earlier. Three months is appropriate for children.

Do people recover from ME?

Yes and no.

People do recover. The prognosis is better for younger sufferers.

However, recovery can be a relative term. The majority of people are forced to learn to live with the varying degrees of symptoms which they retain. Some stay severely ill.

80% of patients do not get better. According to US statistics provided by the Centres for Disease Control (CDC), only 4% of patients had full remission (not recovery) at 24 months.

International expert Daniel Peterson is on record as stating about ME / ICD-CFS:

"In my experience, (it) is one of the most disabling diseases that I care for, far exceeding HIV disease except for the terminal stages".

American researchers found that the quality of life is particularly and uniquely disrupted in ME / ICD-CFS and that all participants related profound and multiple losses, including loss of jobs, relationships, financial security, future plans, daily routines, hobbies, stamina and spontaneity. Activity was reduced to basic survival needs for some subjects. The researchers found that the extent of the losses experienced by sufferers was devastating, both in number and intensity.

Australian researchers found that patients with this disorder had more dysfunction than those with multiple sclerosis, and that in ME / ICD-CFS the degree of impairment is more extreme than in end-stage renal disease and heart disease, and that only in terminally ill cancer and stroke patients was the sickness impact profile (SIP) greater than in ME /ICD-CFS.

This is where bio-medical research is necessary as there are reasons to believe that we are on the threshold of discovering why ME takes a hold.

Invest In M.E are campaigning and fund raising for bio-medical research. It is sad that because we cannot get support from the Government,poorly sufferers have to raise their own funds for the hope of a cure. You can find out more about the clinical trials and ways you can support IIME by visiting their website.

http://www.investinme.org

In loving memory of Maureen Boniface

1945 - 2016

Thank you for believing in me. You told me that you knew I would never give up... and I want you to know, I will never give up.

ABOUT THE AUTHOR

Hayley Green is a 28 year old M.E sufferer in the UK. This is her sixth publication. She suffers from Moderate M.E and is predominantly housebound.

Previous publications include
- 101 Tips For Coping With ME
- What Is M,E? A Guide For Children
- Understanding ME – A Guide For Friends, Family & Carers
- Tickle ME – Stories of a brain fogged girl
- Life With M.E – Words Of Warriors

100% of all royalties from the publications are donated to Invest In M.E to support Bio-medical research

Printed in Great Britain
by Amazon